A Desert Place in The Sea

The Early Churches
of
Northern Lewis

Michael Robson

Comunn Eachdraidh Nis

Comunn Eachdraidh Nis are grateful to the people of Ness for their contribution to this publication.

We acknowledge subsidy from the following towards the cost of publication:

Galson Estate, Colum Cille Anniversary Project (including Leader, Western Isles Council and Western IslesTourist Board)

First published in 1997 by Comunn Eachdraidh Nis, Habost, Ness.

ISBN   0 953137406
Designed by Comunn Eachdraidh Nis.
Printed by the Stornoway Gazette

Contents

Foreword

We are very pleased to be associated with this important publication in the year of the 1400th anniversary of the death of St Columba. The history of the early churches of Lewis has been neglected for far too long and it is appropriate that it has been highlighted at this time. We are greatly indebted to Michael Robson for undertaking the necessary research and for writing the text in such a short time. We also thank the members of our own Management and Archive Committees who helped with the project in various ways. It is our intention to widen the range of our publications during the next few years. We are stewards of a valuable treasury of textual and photographic material which we would like to make available to as large an audience as possible.

Iain G. Macdonald

Chairman
Comunn Eachdraidh Nis

INTRODUCTION:

Forgotten Treasures

It is easy for the road-bound visitor to the north of Lewis to miss the places and objects of greatest interest. The local resident, on the other hand, knowing full well where they are, tends not to bother with them, just as the citizen of Edinburgh rarely sees the inside of the castle which may be in view every day. The sites and visible remains of the ancient churches which were once and may yet be of deep significance to the people living between the village of Shader and the Butt of Lewis, and even beyond the Butt on the lonely island of Rona, are not the least important in the area's long history. Two hundred and more years ago they impressed visitors who had far more difficult travel problems than those of today. Each site now lies only a short walk from a road, except of course Rona and its neighbour Sùla Sgeir!

In 1760 a survey was made of the condition of parishes in the Highlands and islands. Those entrusted with the task were impressed with the lack of up-to-date churches in western districts. 'In almost all these Countrys, where Churches are now wanting', they reported, 'we saw the Ruins of Decent Edifices, which had been antiently devoted to Sacred use. These had been built before the

Reformation. We observe with Concern that Since that period, in many parishes the house of God hath Continued to lye waste'. Educational facilities too were, in their opinion, completely inadequate, an equally disturbing situation as religion and education were then seen to go hand in hand in most parts of Scotland.

At that time the island of Lewis was divided into four parishes, including that of Barvas with Ness. Here a parish kirk and manse actually existed at Barvas itself though there was no officially recognised glebe for the minister. There was also 'another Kirk at Swainbost, twelve miles Distant', for the populous district of Ness was a long way from the Barvas church and needed a more accessible place of worship. And scattered throughout the length of the parish were remains of many 'Decent Edifices, which had been antiently devoted to Sacred use'.

In northern Lewis there are at least eight and perhaps ten of these old buildings, with two or three more on the islands of Rona and Sùla Sgeir. Among them is the 'Kirk at Swainbost' which is certainly of pre-Reformation age and like the others associated with the old Catholic church. They are all located on or very near the sea coast and, except for Luchruban and Sùla Sgeir, close to settlements in which the people made a living from surrounding good land and from fishing. Each of the buildings is known in Gaelic as a 'Teampull', the English for which is not easy to determine. 'Temple' is really inappropriate, while the commonly used 'chapel' is convenient but not universally accurate. 'Church' is preferred here even though this may suggest a larger and grander structure than any 'Teampull' in the area. For reasons not yet explained 'Teampull', derived from Latin, was the word used in northern Lewis, while elsewhere in the islands the common term was 'Cill' which may suggest a stronger Irish connection. The interior of the Teampull when in use cannot have been anything other than bare and uncomfortable with an earth floor, possibly some stone wall benches, a stone font and a simple altar of small stone slabs. Calculations of building size varied considerably, often being no more than the approximations of surveyors and visitors in a hurry; they are recorded in several published accounts, including the Inventory of Monuments (1928) and subsequent 'Sites and Monuments' lists.

However it is translated and whatever its original significance, 'Teampull' does not now reveal anything precise about the age and function of the pre-Reformation church. More helpful in this respect may be the dedication or other name by which a church is distinguished. Martin Martin, in his *Description of the Western Islands of Scotland*, first published in 1703, provided the earliest known list of the old Lewis churches and their dedications, including most of those in the northern part of the island:

'St. *Collum* in *Garieu,* St. *Ronan* in *Eorobie,* St.*Thomas* in *Habost,* St.*Peter* in *Shanabost,* St.*Clemen* in *Dell, Holy-Cross* Church in *Galan,* St.*Brigit* in *Barove,* St.*Peter* in *Shiadir,* St.*Mary* in *Barvas.....'*

Perhaps the first of these to be recorded was 'St. *Mary* in *Barvas'* outside the present 'northern Lewis' district but nevertheless very closely connected with it. 'St. *Collum* in *Garieu'* is probably the 'S. Columba' marked on sixteenth century maps and appearing on at least one of them as 'S. Columban'. This dedication is different from the 'St. Columkil, in the Island of that Name', also given by Martin, and may denote an early forgotten church in Ness. It could be represented by 'Ghearen', a name appearing on Pont's map of Lewis and Harris surveyed around 1600, and placed rather vaguely but somewhere not far from Knockaird. Given the possibility that some dedications of an 'Irish' kind might have preceded those of a familiarly 'Roman' note, the sites of churches of St.

Columba, St. Ronan and St. Bridget might be older than the rest but this can only be speculation.

Small early places of worship such as the cells on Rona, Sùla Sgeir and Luchruban were often founded in remote spots by monks from substantial religious centres like Iona. Courageous figures skilled in the use of sea-going curachs and in means of survival, each sought an isolated place, 'a desert place in the sea'*, where in a hermitage built of stone he could pursue through physical deprivation and through contemplation a purer spiritual state. In other words he undertook the experience of what was called the 'white martyrdom', for which Cormac, a contemporary of Columba, made three long voyages. To appreciate the hardships these people endured it is better to stand on the bare rock of Sùla Sgeir than in the accessible, fertile, machair lands of a place like Eoropie where the church was far larger than the hermit monk's cell and served a different purpose.

It would be wrong to look upon even the larger old churches with conventional preconceptions about parishes, congregations and meetings. Some of these buildings were of a size more suited to a few priestly figures, while only two or three could house a company of local inhabitants, and the relationship of a religious

*A.O. & M.O. Anderson(editor) *Adomnan's Life of Columba* London 1961 p.441

9

presence to a neighbouring community is not at all clear. The earliest foundations had presumably to face up to pagan Norse invaders, but whether they were destroyed or treated with respect is largely unknown in spite of certain instances of slaughter and plunder. In due course Norse settlers were converted to a form of Christianity and might themselves have encouraged the establishment of churches; and the 'Roman' dedications, or re-dedications, of most of the churches in northern Lewis may indicate foundations of a later period still.

The Catholic pattern of church organisation achieved a system of parishes which became the basis of the later, Protestant arrangement. This meant enhanced importance for those existing early places of worship that were turned into parish churches, while most of the rest declined and even fell into ruin. In addition, landowners or other leaders of the population had increasing influence. Some of the latter may indeed have seen to the establishment of small churches on their own ground for their own and for their neighbours' use. It has been remarked that in Orkney 'chapels' can be associated with units of land called *eyrisland* or 'ounceland', a Norse term for ground possessed by a settlement group or an important individual, and it is of interest that at Shader, Melbost and Eoropie the word

Eire occurs in placenames though in these examples it may mean 'beach' rather than an area of land.

The churches of northern Lewis, whatever their origin, eventually stood within the territory of the MacLeods of Lewis who maintained possession of their estate, including the small outlying islands, until the early 1600s. Morrisons, however, are known to have held a strong position in Ness and may themselves have required a place of worship. That some at least of the MacLeod chiefs took religion seriously seems to be illustrated in the permission granted in June 1405 to 'the nobleman Roderic Macleord, baron of Leows', to have a portable altar. Two years earlier there was a reference to the church of St. Mary 'in Barwas' [Barvas], to visitors there on feast days, and to those who made contributions towards maintaining it in repair. St. Mary's in Barvas must have been one of the four parish kirks of Lewis mentioned in 1549, while another was the principal ecclesiastical building in the parish of Ness and to be identified either with Teampull Mholuaidh in Eoropie or, more probably, with Teampull Pheadair in Swainbost.

Even in the 1400s there are records showing that churches in the Western Isles suffered from being remote and from the dangers surrounding them in a period of frequent warfare, so that many lacked priests or monks to serve them. The monastery on Iona was at risk in the 1420s 'because it is situated in the Isles among the wild Scots.....and is almost destroyed in its buildings and rents by continuous wars'. Unless a dominant local figure such as MacLeod of Lewis felt a religious establishment to be important and gave it his protection the church, particularly if small and isolated, was liable to be destroyed in the course of feuds and fights. It might equally well fall into decay through mere neglect and absence of priest or other incumbent.

In spite of such circumstances however the old churches of northern Lewis, as elsewhere, continued to receive the regard of ordinary local people long after they had ceased to function as originally intended. Several examples of this persistent veneration occur in the descriptions that follow, especially in that of Teampull Mholuaidh with which Brand's account of a similar church in Orkney may be compared:

'There are several old Chappels in these Isles, which the People resort unto, but that which I heard of, as the most famous is St. Tredwels Chappel in Papa-Westra, which they have such a Veneration for, that they will come from other Isles in considerable numbers to it, some of us having occasion to be on that Isle, we saw this Chappel, situated on a small low Rock, within a Loch commonly called St. Tredwels Loch, to which we passed by stepping-stones, before this Chappel door there was a heap of small stones, into which the Superstitious People when they come, do cast a small stone or two for their offering, and some will cast in Money; the Chappel hath been but little, and is now Ruinous, only some of the Walls are standing, which the People are so far from suffering to be demolished, that they labour to keep them up, and tho the Proprietour of the ground hath some way enclosed it, yet this proves not effectual to prevent the frequenting thereof.'

Brand, like Martin Martin, was writing around 1700 and with a familiar, Protestant point of view. People still went to St. Tredwel's Loch for cures much as they did to Teampull Mholuaidh and still frequented other ancient churches for prayer and 'Superstitious Practices'. Strong adherence to old religious customs associated with the Celtic as well as the Norwegian church was as marked in

Orkney, and Shetland, as in Lewis; 'And tho' their Ministers both privately and publickly have spoken to them, yet they cannot get them to forbear and abandon these Customs'. Antiquity and long practice had firmly embedded the sanctity of both church and custom in the minds and hearts of those who looked upon the fallen walls, and there were stories in the Northern Isles which relate as much to Teampull na Crò Naomh at Galson as to the thirty-five or more 'little Chappels' in Unst and Yell:

> 'These are said to have been built by Superstitious Zealots in the times of Popery, or as some rather think by Ship-wrackt Seamen, who coming safe to shore, have Built them according to their Vows made by them when in danger, which they dedicated to many several Saints, whom they looked upon as the Patrons of their Respective Chappels.'

It is perhaps as difficult now to discover when the old Lewis churches were abandoned as to fix upon the times when they were built. But it is clear that although eighteenth century Protestant ministers took measures 'for the eradicating and utter abolishing of these Relicts of Paganism and Idolatry' the little buildings, however ruinous, on the rainy headlands and sandy lands of the west have retained their power over the imagination and their ability to claim veneration and respect.

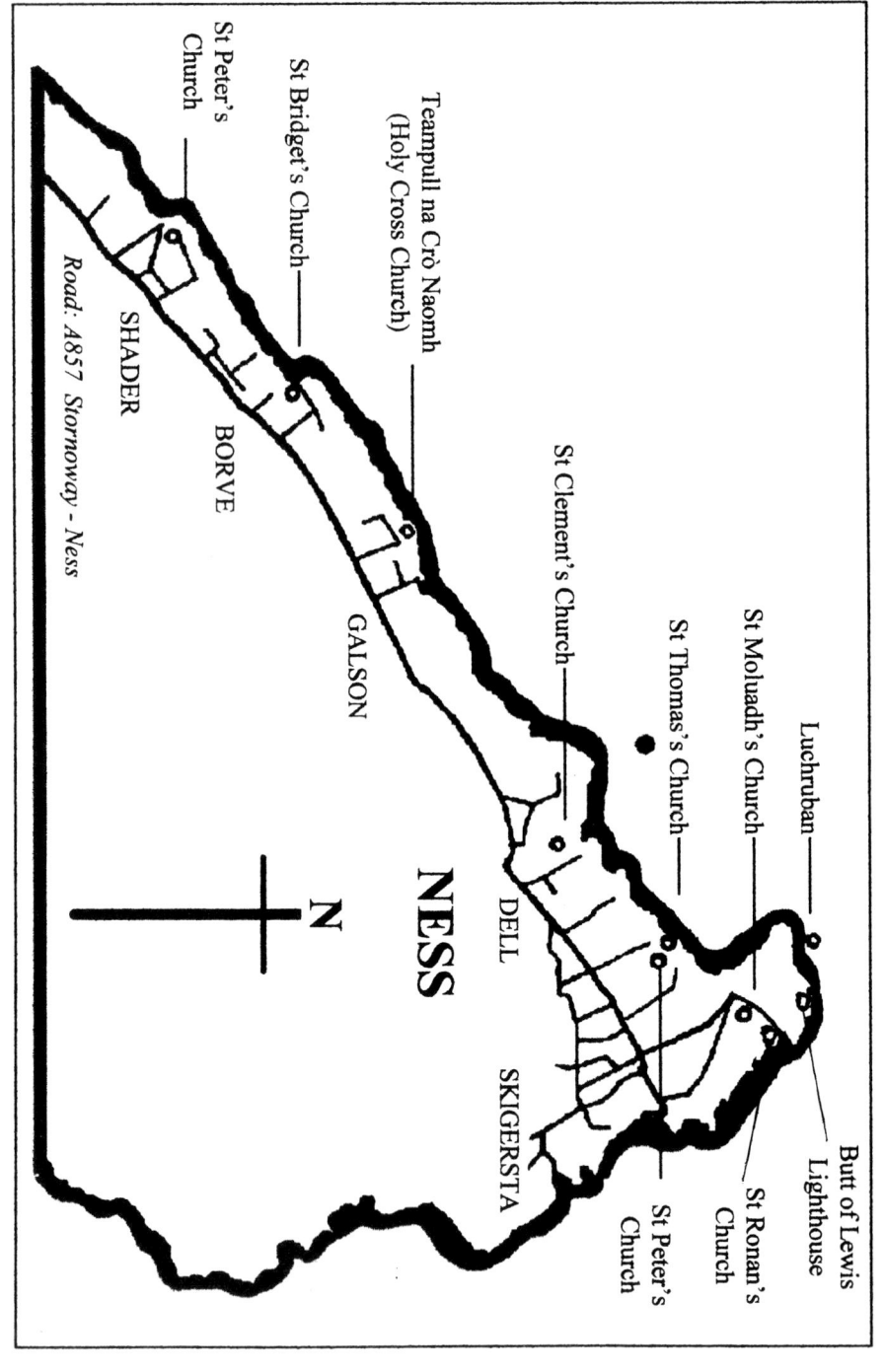

St Peter's Church

St Bridget's Church

Teampull na Crò Naomh (Holy Cross Church)

St Clement's Church

Luchruban

St Moluadh's Church

St Thomas's Church

Butt of Lewis Lighthouse

St Ronan's Church

St Peter's Church

SHADER

BORVE

GALSON

DELL

SKIGERSTA

NESS

N

Road: A857 Stornoway - Ness

Chapter 1

LUCHRUBAN

In the extreme north-west of the Ness district is Luchruban. It appears on Pont's map of about 1600 as 'Ylen Dunibeg' which in English is 'Island of Little Men'. Today the significance of the name survives in the Ness phrase 'bodaich bheaga Luchrubain', 'the little men of Luchruban'. In spite of various conjectures regarding little people and equivalents in Irish the placename remains something of a mystery, though Martin, writing around 1700, produced one explanation. He said that in 'a Tradition which the Natives have of a very Low-statur'd People living once here' the word 'Lusbirdan', meaning 'Pigmies', was used, while the 'Natives' themselves called the place *'The Island of Little Men'*

The notion of pigmies was first recorded in Monro's account of 1549:

'At the north point of Leozus thair is ane little Ile callit the *Pygmeis Ile*, with ane little kirk in it of thair awn handie wark. Within this kirk the ancients of the cuntrie of Leozus sayis that the saids Pygmeis hes bene earthit [buried] thair. Mony men of divers cuntries

17

hes delvit up deiply the fluir of the said kirk, and I myself amangis the lave [rest], and hes fundin in it deip under the earth certane banes and round heids of verie little quantitie, alledgit to be the banes of the saids Pygmeis, quhilk may be licklie according to sindrie storeis that we reid of the Pygmeis. But I leave this far of it to the ancients of the Leozus.'

An account of about 1580 is a little more positive:

'In this Ile [Lewis] thair is ane little Cove biggit in form of ane kirk, and is callit the Pygmies Kirk. It is sa little, that ane man may scairslie stand uprichtlie in it eftir he is gane in on his kneis. Thair is sum of the Pygmies banes thairinto as yit, of the quhilkis the thrie [i.e. thie (thigh)] banes being measurit is not fullie twa inches lang.'

It is possible of course that this description was merely an inventive reworking of Monro's. About fifty years later Captain Dymes showed that he was not convinced by the story of the little men. He saw 'the Pygmeys Island' as 'a round high hill.....wherein there is the walls of a Chappell to bee seene wch is but 8 foote in length and 6 foote in breadth, the ground whereof hath bene often tymes digged vpp espetially by the Irish wch come thither of purpose to gett the bones of those little people wch they say were buryed there'. Dymes, like Monro, explored the site himself. 'At my beinge vpon the Ile I made search in the earth and found some of those bones'. They were so small that he felt it unlikely that they came from any sort of human being. If by 'the Irish' Dymes meant people from Ireland as W C. MacKenzie preferred to think then it may be wondered why they came all that way in order to look for little bones; but it is possible that 'the Irish' were really Gaelic-speaking local inhabitants.

Monro said that little men were buried on the island, Martin that they lived there; John Morison, tacksman of South Bragar, who was born about the year that Dymes wrote his description of Lewis, had no great faith in the origin of the little bones either:

'There is a little Island hard by the coast where it is said that Pigmeis lived some tyme by reason they find by searching some small bons in the earth; but I can not give much faith to it, since greater mans bons would consume in a shorter tyme but I hold them to be the bons of small foulls which abound in that place.'

Morison's comments were made in the early 1680s, not long before Martin Martin's own account, and they are as sensible as any. Bones found on Luchruban two centuries later were sent by MacKenzie to the Natural History Museum in London where they were identified as those of animals and birds.

Today, however, the pigmy story persists, and there are still visible remains of sunken structures contained within a roughly circular or oval area dreadfully exposed to wind and spray. Whether the walls are those of dwelling,

The ruins of the cell on Luchruban. c. 1920 © RCAHMS

monastic cell or 'kirk' is unknown. A survey in July 1921 recorded measurements of 'chambers' and described the whole as 'a peculiar construction'. For over four hundred years visitors of many kinds have dug within the ruined walls and have found fragments of unglazed and mostly undecorated pottery as well as pieces of bone, but each such excavation has merely increased the confused and confusing state of Monro's 'kirk'.

The tone of MacKenzie's writings on 'the Pigmies Isle' suggests that his acquaintance with the district was limited. His attention seems to have been concentrated on showing that the existence of 'pigmies' could be separated from the discovery of small bones and that the 'little men' of Luchruban might be similar to other northern peoples such as Laplanders. Whether or not the plan and measurements of the site he provided were accurate, perhaps his most valuable contribution was his brief outline of traditions relating to the little men. The first concerned a holy man or 'saint' called Frangus. 'St. Frangus', he noted, 'is said to have been an outlaw who lived on the sands of Lionel at Ness. According to the tradition, which was recently taken down from the lips of an old resident of Ness, Frangus was unkind to the pigmies, who hanged him on a hill, which is called *Bruich Frangus* to this day'. The second concerned the little men themselves. 'They are said to have been "Spaniards", who came to Lewis 500 years B.C. In the year 1 A.D. "big yellow men" came from Argyll and drove the little men from Cunndal (a cove near Luchruban) to the latter island; but when the pigmies got numerous they emigrated to Europie and Knockaird in the same vicinity. They lived on "buffaloes" which they killed by throwing "sharp-pointed knives at them" '. Since the 'old resident of Ness' must have spoken in Gaelic, the use of the word 'buffaloes' seems inappropriate and illustrates the superficial and sketchy way in which these traditions are presented. In addition the word 'cove' should apparently have been 'cave', though neither is suitable for Cunndal, which is a broad, open bay. It is of interest however that some of the bones that have been found on Luchruban are those of an ox.

In the course of a visit to the Cunndal area MacKenzie 'discovered some twenty-five or more hut-circles, with stone foundations in, I think, one instance only, the others being simply mounds of turf'. According to 'information in the district' seaweed-storing and fish-curing were associated with these remains, which, it was learned on 'further inquiry', had 'existed "from time immemorial"', and, according to the old Ness man, they had formed the dwellings of his pigmies previous to their migration to Luchruban'. MacKenzie evidently liked to give the impression of making discoveries - 'I am glad to have re-discovered the Pigmies Isle' - but of course Luchruban had never been lost and the curious circle of linked mounds not far back from the cliff edge at Cunndal had long been obvious and is still very distinct. Perhaps the link, if there is one, between the two locations has more to do with the 'kirk' than with 'pigmies'.

The site of St Ronan's Church from Stoth. The church used to stand on the highest point on the horizon. © Donna Scott.

Chapter 2

ST. RONAN'S CHURCH

A mile to the east of Luchruban and a few hundred yards from the Butt of Lewis is the small inlet of Stoth. Sheltered from the west when the wind is not very strong, Stoth was an ancient landing place, used long ago by the Norsemen and by the boats going between Lewis and the distant island of Rona. In more recent times materials for building the lighthouse were brought ashore there, as were supplies for the lighthouse and the keepers thereafter. After landing and before departure Rona people were said in tradition to have made their way past Clach Eireisgean to the top of the hill sloping up gently from Stoth. Here they prayed at a church called Teampull Rònain, or sometimes, Teampull Rònaidh. Martin called it 'St. *Ronan* in *Eorobie'* but gave no further information.

Very little is known about this church which in some ways is rather overshadowed by the nearby 'Church of St.*Mulvay* ', Teampull Mholuaidh, and, more remotely, by the cell on Rona with which it was linked through the apparent dedication as well as in tradition. Few traces remain, and the Ordnance Survey did not even accept that it had been a religious building at all although the surveyor was given 'Teampull Rònaidh' as its name:

'The ruins of a small hut, on the summit of an arable Knoll, at the Butt of Lewis. It is about 20 feet long, by 12 wide, and is supposed to be of great Antiquity. It is said to have been built by a person named Ronaidh, who with his Sister inhabited it. The Supposition that it was a Church, appears to be fabulous, as it is not borne out by either tradition or appearance. No part of the walls is now Standing.'

About ten years after the Survey T.S. Muir discerned a shape in the uneven turf which he described in 1861 as 'the ground-work of Teampull Rona, a building which is traditionally regarded and spoken of by the Butt people, as having been of much older date than any of the religious houses in northern Lewis'. As for its shape and size he could only guess: 'It seems to have been of the ordinary rectangular shape, and about thirty feet in length'. Today the site is not much altered, except that the network of croft fences makes it a little more difficult to reach.

Chapter 3

THE CHURCH ON RONA

In describing St. Ronan's church in Ness Michael Hayes of the Ordnance Survey remarked that the island of Rona, forty miles north or north-east of the Butt, also received its name from the same saint, 'who with his Sister visited it on the back of a large Whale'.

Although the island may have been called Rona for a quite different reason these few words show that Hayes had been told, perhaps in outline, the lengthy story of how 'St. Ronan' and possibly two sisters left Ness not on a whale but with the divinely-sent help of a great sea creature known as the 'cìonaran-crò'. On reaching the island the holy man jumped ashore, his sudden arrival causing all the evil creatures that inhabited the place to leave by sliding down slabs of rock into the ocean. According to the story at least one cell was built and presumably a dwelling, and far from being mere visitors 'St. Ronan' and his sisters became residents, the saint himself spending the rest of his life there. A stone, roughly shaped into a cross, was said to have marked his grave.

The Church on Rona. c. 1924 On the extreme right is the 3 holed cross now held in Comunn Eachdraidh Nis. © RCAHMS.

A 'village' settlement was established on Rona, and the visitors from the Ordnance Survey had much more to record than the tale briefly mentioned by Hayes.

'There are a graveyard and Church......attached to the village. The former is enclosed by a wall composed of Stone and Earth and contains in or about its centre a rude stone cross without any inscription. The latter is on the south side of the former and is about 7 yards long by 4 yards wide. The walls are still standing and are about 6 feet high, and composed of stone and lime. There is a small house at its S. East end, which appears to have been formerly used as a vestry as it communicates with the Church by means of a small door or opening. Its walls are built of lime and stone and roofed with the same materials. It is about 6 feet long, four feet wide and about 8 feet high. It is plastered and whitewashed with lime on the inside which keeps it dry and prevents it from being in ruins like the others.'

Descriptions of these religious remains vary but all agree

that there were two parts to the 'chapel'. Visiting the island in 1857 and 1860, soon after the surveyors, T. S. Muir interpreted the parts as 'cell' and 'nave'. He could not put a date on either but the former 'is certainly by many hundred years the older erection, and in all probability the work of the eighth or ninth century'.

'Of this rude and diminutive building not much can be said. On the outside, it is in most part a rounded heap of loose stones, roofed over with turf. Within, you find it a roughly-built cell, 9 ft. 3 in. in height, and at the floor 11 ft. 6 in. long and 7 ft. 6 in. wide. The end walls lean inwardly a little, the side ones so greatly that, where they meet the flat slab-formed roof, they are scarcely two feet apart. Beyond the singularity of its shape, there is nothing remarkable in the building, its only minute features being a square doorway in the west end, so low that you have to creep through it on your elbows and knees; a flat-headed window, without splay on either side, 19 in. long and 8 in. wide, set over the doorway; another window of like form and length, but an inch or two wider, near the east end of the south wall; and the altar-stone, 3 ft. in length, lying close to the east end.'

Of the other part Muir had this to say:

'Attached as a nave to the west end of the cell, and externally coextensive with it in breadth, are the remains of another chapel, internally 14 ft. 8 in. in length, and 8 ft. 3 in. in width. Except the north one, which is considerably broken down, all the elevations are nearly entire, the west one retaining a part of the gable. A rude flat-headed doorway, 3 ft. 5 in. in height, and 2 ft. 3 in. wide, in the south wall, and a small window of the same shape, eastward of it, are the only details.'

He had little to add to what the surveyors had noted about the graveyard:

'In the burying-ground, which is fenced by a low wall, with a doorway on the south-west, there are several truncated plain stone crosses, the tallest one only 2 ft. 6 in. in height. At the intersection of the arms it is pierced with a triangular group of three small round holes, touching which, as also the pillar itself, there is a variously-told tradition among those of the Butt.'

Unfortunately Muir did not at this point provide the tradition.

Surveyors of ancient and historical monuments came in 1924 and shared the view that 'the eastern division' of the 'church' was 'manifestly much older than the western division'. They thought it might have been 'an early, possibly Celtic, chapel', serving later 'as a chancel to the western portion or nave'. This opinion would contradict Muir's comment that there was nothing remarkable about the building, for it stands out as quite exceptional in the Western Isles. Again measurements differed and no trace was found in the cell 'of an eastern window or of an altar slab'. Over the past sixty years further decay of the walls had taken place. Today, however, the visitor might be impressed with the degree of survival in something so ancient, a situation that may have resulted from the isolation of the setting and from the restoration work carried out at various times. Nevertheless, weathering continues and there has been a further major collapse of stonework.

The two sections of building were both present when Dean Monro recorded information about the island in 1549:

'Within this Ile thair is ane chapell callit St. Ronans Chapell, into the quhilk chapell (as the ancients of that cuntrie alledgis) thay use to leave ane spaid and ane schoole [shovel] quhan ony deid, and upon the morn findis the place of the grave taiknit with ane spaid (as thai alledge).'

This seems to be the earliest mention of both church and burial ground, and there can be no doubt that 'the ancients' or old people could have told a great deal more. For instance they did not refer to a second cell. In spite of Muir's reference to the so-called nave as 'another chapel' it would appear from tradition and from what Muir himself was told that a second cell, if there was one, was quite separate from 'St. Ronan's'. The saint was said to have built for one of his sisters a church or cell called after her Teampull Mhionagain or Teampull Mhiriceil. An account of about 1680 noted that 'In this Ronay there are tuo little cheapels where Sanct Ronan lived all his tym as ane heremite'; and in a letter to Muir about 1860 the tenant of Rona, Daniel Murray, made remarks about

Angus Gunn, whose story of the saint's journey to the island on the 'cìonaran-crò' was followed with information on what may be called the second cell although it was now given a different name and origin.

The entrance to St Ronan's cell. © F. Fraser Darling collection.

'It was this Ronan that built the east end of the present teampull, or the part that still stands of it. After him, Roman Catholics occupied the island, and they built another teampull which was called *Teampull nam Manach*. It was outside the grave-yard, and about 15 yards from the east end of the present teampull; it was roofed with timber and thatched with straw, and was about the size of the west end of the present temple, with an altar in the middle 4 feet square by 3 feet high, and having a round gray stone on the top. The roof and part of the wall was pulled down four hundred years since, but the altar and part of the wall (3 feet in height) were standing when Angus Gunn was on the island.....'

It is possible that 'Teampull nam Manach', church of the monks, was the same as Teampull Mhionagain, but by the time Murray wrote his letter it had long been forgotten, except by Angus Gunn who was not able to show Muir where it had stood.

The old Catholic religion persisted among the Rona people many years after the Reformation. In another account of the late seventeenth century long-established religious practices, different from that involving spade and grave, were described:

'There is a chappel in the midst of the Isle, where they meet twice or thrice a day. One of the families is hereditary Bedell and the Master of that stands at the Altar and prayeth; the rest kneel upon their knees, and joyn with him. Their Religion is the Romish Religion.'

The people who met there were the Rona people, of whose origin nothing is known, and they had apparently maintained the 'nave' and cell as a church in which to worship. When at about the same time Rev. Donald Morison, the Protestant minister of Barvas parish to which Ness and Rona were then attached, made a visit to the island he saw 'a chapel dedicated to St. Ronan, fenced with a stone-wall round it' in which the islanders congregated for services. He found it neatly cared for, as it was swept clean each day, and on the altar lay a plank of wood about ten feet long - 'every foot has a hole in it, and in every hole a stone, to which the natives ascribe several virtues.....'. One of these stones was particularly effective in 'promoting speedy delivery to a woman in travail'. Morison also learned that every Sunday morning the people assembled in the church and repeated the Lord's Prayer, the Creed, and the Ten Commandments.

Not long after this the old native population of Rona died out, and though the island was again inhabited by families from Lewis the significance of the 'church' was never quite the same. It continued to be regarded as a sacred place of worship, and certain rituals and customs were still practised, but full recognition of what these things meant was missing, just as modern thought tends to dismiss the old tales of men like Angus Gunn instead of seeking to understand them.

By Muir's time, in the mid nineteenth century, Rona was finally deserted and abandoned as a place of permanent settlement. The cell, over a thousand years old, and its accompanying 'nave' were already falling into ruin. The cell had a gaping hole in the eastern end, and Muir's informant, John MacKay, son of a former resident, had heard that the Ordnance Survey was responsible:

> '....I was told that the Sappers, when on the island measuring it, or doing something or other there........made a hole in the teampull, at one end of it, just between the roof and the wall; and I did see that stones had been taken out of it there, as I was looking round it.....May be you don't believe it; but some of the Ness men, who were over to clip the sheep, told me they saw them do it, because they wanted to know what sort of place it was inside, but couldn't make up their minds to the trouble of going in by the door.'

The trouble with the proper entrance to the cell was that the doorway had silted up with earth and other debris, and it was only possible to get through by crawling 'on your elbows and knees'. And so the whole building, with its two parts, looked as if at last time had caught up with it. Eventually, in the late 1930s, the passage was dug clear and the entrance to the 'nave' from outside, together with a piece of walling, was reconstructed, while the hole in the cell was repaired in 1959. Whether or not it was right to do this was a subject raised forty years earlier in the report of an excursion made by antiquarians in 1899.

'It is not yet too late to have these most interesting structures properly conserved. Restoration or building up a new St. Ronan's Church is not suggested, only the replacing of the stones in the same position as indicated in Mr. Muir's sketches. His ground plan is practically correct, and there is internal evidence that the elevation of the small cell interior, as represented......is a correct drawing. The actual cost of providing the necessary labour for this purpose, that is, bringing the men from the mainland and housing them on the island, would not be very great; no doubt some competent archaeologist could be found willing to incur the expense of visiting the place to supervise the work. Without such supervision it would be better not to touch the remains.'

Much of Rona's history is unknown and many features await the attention of more than one 'competent archaeologist'. East of the cell is a site which may contain evidence of the second 'church'. Close round the whole present 'church' there appears to be the mound of an enclosing wall, and within the wider area of the burial ground may be the traces of other buildings as well as numbers of as yet undiscovered tombstones. Angus

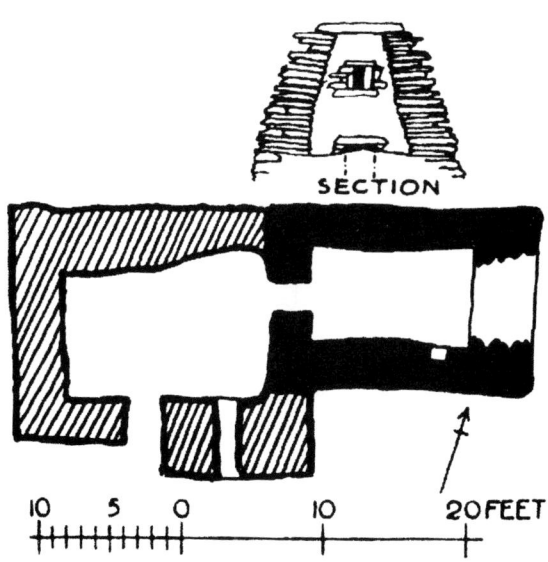

T.S. Muir's plan of the church on Rona. Old Church Architecture 1861.

Gunn remembered that he had seen stones in the shape of a cross or with a cross cut on them, and 'There were carved burial stones there too with swords and shields and crosses thereon; but they got broken and lost and most have disappeared'. One or two of these stones were taken into the roofless 'nave' , one or two more were left amid the grass along with numerous rough, unmarked stones such as are to be found in most Hebridean graveyards. As burials in the ground by St. Ronan's chapel scarcely occurred at all after the beginning of the nineteenth century, it would seem that the majority of surviving stones may reflect the deaths of that 'ancient race' that came to an end about 1700. Muir's three-holed stone, which was said to be the gravestone of St Ronan himself, was believed to be otherwise unmarked and still lacks a proper explanatory description. The 1899 antiquarians, most of them from Ireland, were more observant than Muir as regards the stone for an incomplete drawing was made of a male human figure carved on one side. This stone was removed from Rona over sixty years ago and can now, fortunately, be seen in the more accessible setting of the Ness Historical Society premises in Habost.

Stones have gone missing and church walls have fallen, but the oldest stone and the oldest building, both perhaps associated immediately with the saint who left Ness long ago for 'a desert place in the sea' survive in worn and moving completeness. From the first the presence of the holy man can be felt, and in the midst of the cell, with its small stone altar and bare walls, his kneeling figure still has its place amid the austere and haunting silence. On Rona, occupied only by birds and seals, the essence of all the ancient churches is most alive.

Chapter 4

THE CELL ON SULA SGEIR

Sùla Sgeir, eleven miles or so west of Rona, is a long rock rising over two hundred feet from the sea. There is little vegetation, not much depth of soil where there is any, and no spring of fresh water, but in summer there are great numbers of seabirds. It is hard to imagine that anyone could ever have lived there for long or that a place of worship would be built in such an outlandish situation.

T.S Muir's drawing of the cell on Sùla Sgeir. Old Church Architecture 1861

None of the early accounts of the Western Isles mention a cell on Sùla Sgeir. But when in October 1850 Miles Carbery of the Ordnance Survey arrived there he discovered that there were several huts grouped together about the middle of the island: 'One of the oldest and apparently largest of these, they call the Temple'. The word 'Teampull' also occurred in 'Sgoir an Teampull', the name of a 'bold rocky point of land' on the east side reached by crossing a narrow neck on which the 'teampull' itself was built. There was therefore already a structure known as a place of worship before the mid nineteenth century.

T.S. Muir, exploring the rock in 1860, came to a 'Comparatively level spot closely surrounded by rocks' where he found a 'low rough, oval-shaped chapel', which he also described as 'a low rugged building with rounded corners and curved roof, called *Tigh Beannaichte* (Blessed House)'. Although it would seem from this that he was told this name he was later supposed to have invented it, but whether he did so or not he was in no doubt as to its 'extreme antiquity': 'Externally, the building is a little dilapidated at both ends, and so is the roof; but within, it is quite perfect, and seemingly no ways altered from its original state.' Entrance was by 'a low and very narrow flat-topped doorway with sloping jambs, in the south wall'; to the east of this was 'a small square-shaped niche' and another recess of the same kind was near the north end of the west wall. The only window was a small square one at the east end above an altar stone 'flanked by slabs set on edge and raised on a slightly elevated dais'.

No-one else provided any other kind of evidence for the existence of a 'church' on Sùla Sgeir and the surveyors of the ancient and historical monuments in the isles who were at Rona in 1924 never reached the more inaccessible island. Disagreement continued among visitors over whether the structure was a cell at all or just another 'bothy' in which Ness men had lived when there for birds. It was even said that the 'teampull' was a building used as a place of worship by the fowling parties, although there appears to be no evidence for this, whereas the existence of an altar stone as well as of the tradition and the placenames, and the exposed site some way from the other buildings, might support Muir's impression of an ancient 'chapel'. The matter is still undecided. Another curious feature of the 'church' is that, judging from an excavation by two Ness men in 1969, a shaft similar to that towards the northern tip of Sùla Sgeir may descend from beside the altar possibly as far as the roof of the

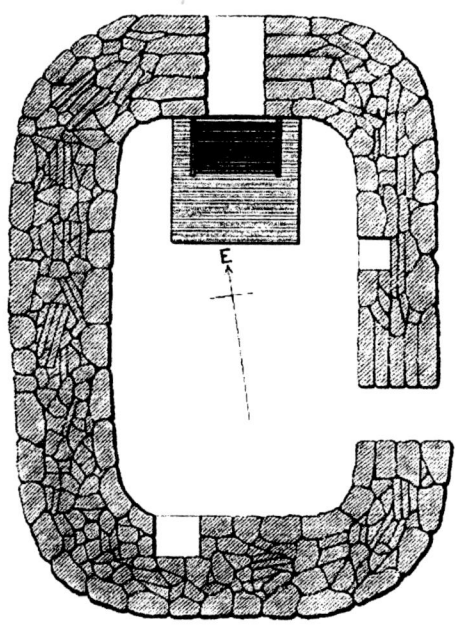

T.S. Muir's plan of the cell on Sùla Sgeir. Old Church Architecture 1861

natural sea tunnel below, though it is now blocked up with loose stones and earth. In recent years the 'church' roof has collapsed.

Tradition certainly continues to accept 'Teampull Shùla Sgeir' as ancient though it does not preserve a dedication. Muir wrote:

> 'Among the Butt people, who all can tell you so much more or less of Saint Ronan, I have not been able to find any legend regarding the holy man who founded the Sula Sgeir teampull and kept ward at its altar. Whoever he was, he was surely a hero.'

These words however reveal the dilemma posed by a lack of written historical record and show a degree of confusion between a dedication and an individual. Among the churches of northern Lewis, most of them dedicated conventionally to saints such as St. Peter and St. Thomas, only one, St. Ronan's at Eoropie, has an association with an individual about whom something is traditionally known. It was therefore not necessary - though understandable - for Muir to regret his failure 'to find any legend' since it would have been highly unusual if he had found one. But there were in fact traditions linking certain individuals of a religious, or at least semi-religious, sort with the island if not with the cell, even though Muir may have heard nothing of them.

The Ordnance Survey was again the first to record a story about one of these mysterious people. Miles Carbery heard it from Donald MacLeod, Ness, who was with him to provide placenames:

'Tradition says that about two hundred years ago, a man of the name of Muldona[c]h was transported from Rona to Sulisgear, and, after an interval of five or six weeks he was found dead from the want [of] Sustenance.'

A dwelling occupied by this man went by the name of 'Tigh Muldonich' according to Donald MacLeod while others thought the spelling would be 'Tigh Mhaoldonuich'. The name was reckoned to mean, for some unknown reason, 'Ludovick's House', though a more likely interpretation in either case would be 'the monk's house'. Whoever he was, the man had little enough space in which to live, even for a few weeks. His rough shelter was 'A small house or hut built of stone. It is about four feet long, three feet wide and three feet high, and supposed to have been the residence of a man who it is said was transported from Rona to Suilisgear for sheep stealing'. He was found dead when the boat came to end his sentence by fetching him back.

Commentary on this tradition might well suggest that certain parts of it were intended to explain the presence of a lone person on Sùla Sgeir. The 'sheep stealing', for instance, might be reasonably thought to account for his exile from Rona, while 'two hundred years ago' might merely mean 'in the distant past'. There is no doubt however that 'Tigh Muldonich' was not the same as 'Teampull Shùla Sgeir', in spite of the monastic significance of the name.

The second individual was the subject of a tale known, as

most Ness stories and traditions were, to Angus Gunn, North Dell. The person is understood to have been a woman called Brianuilt or Brenhilda, one of the sisters of St. Ronan who were with him in Rona, and whose name was evidently of some special note in the northern district of Lewis. According to J.W. Dougal's description of a visit to Sùla Sgeir in the late 1920s it used to be customary for Ness people to refer to the gannet as 'Brenhilda's, or Brianuilte's bird'. Part of the story of how Brianuilt went to Sùla Sgeir was told by Dougal, but he avoided mentioning the reason for her leaving Rona. Angus Gunn gave the reason; one day as Ronan and Brianuilt were returning up Leathad Fianuis on Rona the former admired his sister's beautiful appearance, and as a consequence she felt it would be wise to leave. Somehow she reached Sùla Sgeir, from which she could still see Rona and picture her brother there. Names such as 'Suidhe Bhrianuilt', 'Càrnan Lochan an t-Suidhe' and 'Bealach an t-Suidhe' refer to the place where she sat to gaze across to Rona, and near that seat of stone her skeleton was eventually found with a shag's nest within the breastbone. At the end of his version of the story Dougal wrote 'We have seen Brenhilda's sitting stone in Sulisgeir, and were deeply stirred by it; and we can look at the picture we took of it, with the shadow across the pool, and regard it till time fails.'

The same might well be said of the 'teampull' on its little platform above the arch at Toll Circean, a solitary house of prayer on a wild and stormy rock, so positioned as to be virtually invisible from the sea.

Chapter 5

THE CHURCH AT EOROPIE

Second Corporal Michael Hayes of the Ordnance Survey came to Eoropie in May 1852. He had with him as a guide John Morrison, Knockaird, from whom he recorded the placenames around the village. They reached the ruins of a 'Church' some distance northwards from the village houses and the name of 'Teampull Fo'Luith' was noted, along with a suitable description:

'A plain stone building, with Gables, the four walls of which are still standing and not much decayed. It had four windows, two on the sides, and two on the Ends, and is one of [the] largest ruins of churches in Lewis Island. There is very little known regarding it Except that it is considered very old, and remains under the protection of some Saint or Angel, by whose power, or through whose intercession, Insane people who sleep in it one night are restored to their Senses. The Experiment they say was successfully made a few years ago by an Uig man.'

That the 'church' was comparatively large and widely known for traditions associated with it there is no doubt. The various accounts agree on that; but they differ on matters such as the form of the name and the supposed age of the building.

'Fo'Luith' seems to have been a rendering of the sound heard by the surveyor, for different spellings or versions occur in other records, all of them possibly derived from the personal name Moluag or Moluoc borne by a holy man who was a contemporary of Columba and chiefly associated with the island of Lismore. Irish annals note 'The death of Lugaid of Lismore, that is, Moluoc' in 592, almost the only known historical fact about him. It would seem that 'Moluag' or 'Moluoc' is an affectionate form of 'Lugaid'; and the name occurs in church dedications from Kintyre to the north of Skye as well as further east.

As for its age, Angus Gunn, North Dell, gave the impression that the church in Eoropie, often called Teampull Mholuaidh, was both the first built in Ness and later than its companion churches in the district. This may have been because a second building, perhaps of the fourteenth century, was erected on the site of a more ancient one. In the late 1860s Alexander Carmichael took down from Angus a tale which described the church's origin:

'The Scandinavians were wild people, without compassion, without mercy, without the love of God, without the fear of man. They were wild as wolves and merciless as bears, and murdered and killed and robbed and plundered wherever they went. They came down upon these coasts, slaying the people in their houses and the saints at their altars, burning churches, killing the living and desecrating the dead.

A son of the King of Scandinavia became a good man and wishing to perform good deeds for the evil deeds he had done he built a church down at Rudh Eorapaidh and called it Teampull Mholuag.........the walls of which are still entire. When the walls of the temple were built, the King's son had no roof to put on and he was in great straits. He did not know in all the living world what to do for a roof for the weather was so stormy that his father's galleys could not go to Lochlan [Norway] for wood to make a roof. The prince prayed and prayed, and when he prayed his best a voice came to him in a dream of the night and told him to go to the Stoth and he would find a roof then. The prince arose and went down to the Stoth and there he found a roof floating in the pool prepared and of the size required for his temple. The roof was taken up and placed on the walls of the building which it filled.'

In addition to the church at least two more buildings of importance stood in or near Eoropie. One was 'Caisteal Mhànuis', the castle of Magnus, 'near the well between Eorobe and Habost'. It was said to have been occupied by representatives of King Magnus of Lochlan, and the King himself was understood to have lived and died there. It is likely that this was the stronghold which the minister of Barvas parish, writing in the 1790s, noticed in describing local antiquities: 'a small mount, which evidently bears the mark of having once a building upon it, called *Caistel Olgre, (i.e.)* Olaus his Castle.' This castle was 'Some hundred yards to the south' of a second defensive building closer to the south side of the church, for also from Lochlan had come the first of the MacLeods, who built a 'house' with an iron rampart called 'MacLeod's Castle'. The gate that gave access to this

Teampull Mholuaidh. © Donna Scott.

castle survived at the end of the eighteenth century as 'a piece of wall standing, called.....Macleod's Gate'. A century later, in 1898, 'Geata MhicLeoid' was known to have been 'standing within living memory' but by 1818 the stones from 'Caisteal Mhanuis' or 'Caisteal Olgre' had been removed for the construction of a schoolhouse at Lionel, and earlier still, before 1800, much of the stonework of MacLeod's Castle and Gate had been 'carried away by the tenants for building their houses'.

One of the main reasons why Teampull Mholuaidh became so well known is that from the very beginning it attracted stories and beliefs of a remarkable kind. However, its early association, in tradition, with the MacLeods and the Norwegians suggests that it may have served as a place of worship for the most powerful figures in the area, leaders perhaps newly converted to the Christian religion, although this does not in itself explain the dedication to St. Moluag. The name 'Olgre' in 'Caisteal Olgre', translated into English as 'Olaus', must be a version of 'Olghair', the Gaelic equivalent of the Norse 'Olvir', ancestor of the MacLeods, and in this way some support is given to the tradition of the Eoropie castles. But the statement by MacKenzie that the church was 'commonly called St. Olaf, from its founder' surely reflects the mistaken interpretation of 'Olaus' as 'Olaf' while at the same time strengthening the likelihood of a MacLeod connection. Given the Norse occupation of Ness, however, it is possible that there was for a while an association with St. Olaf, the principal Nordic saint, to whom there were at least eight dedications in Shetland.

Teampull Mholuaidh was generally known as Teampull Mòr, the big church, perhaps because it held the position of greatest significance among other such churches as may have existed in northern Lewis in days before Teampull Pheadair was built at Swainbost. It may also have been the largest of these churches. Situated in green, fertile land now enclosed by croft fences, it was more than just a place of worship to the people in the island who came to respect it. Nearby on its east side a very small run of water called 'Uisge na Comhraiche' marked the boundary of a sanctuary, with which Cnoc Fianuis now in Knockaird village and Cnoc a' Bheannaich near Leistean at the north end of Tràigh Shanndaigh may be associated. According to a tradition MacLeod of Eoropie erected a cross on a small hill at South Dell where there is an enclosed space known still as Buaile na Crois, and introduced a law which stated that the whole of Ness north of the cross was to be the sanctuary. This great area proved to be too large and he had to move the cross nearer to 'Uisge na Comhraiche'. Angus Gunn maintained that it was owing to this law that there came to be so many different 'surnames' in Ness and especially in Eoropie; and those who took advantage of this law as refugees, were said to have come in the 'fate of a red hand' -'Ann am Freasdaill lamh-dhearg'.

In another story it is related that the church was originally on the other side of 'Uisge na Comhraiche'; ' but, in consequence of the heathenish conduct of some of the matrons in its immediate neighbourhood, who, regardless of their proximity to the sacred shrine, continued carding and spinning black wool, with daring impiety, late on a Saturday night' the outraged building 'changed its quarters during the night, and placed running water - "uisge ruith" - between itself and its profane neighbours'. It was indeed a 'temple' of character.

The best known of the beliefs linked to the Teampull Mholuaidh was described first in 1630 by the far from impartial Captain Dymes, who seems to have rather looked down on the Lewis people and their customs and whose version of the church dedication differs from the others. 'In theire religion,' he said, 'they are very ignorant and have been given to the idolatrous worshipp of divers Saints as doth appeare by theire Chappells which are yett to bee seene, but they are nowe most espetially devoted to one of theire Saints called St. Mallonuy whose Chappell is seated in the north part of the Ile, whome they have in great veneration to this daie and keepe the Chappell in good repaire.' The respect with which the church was viewed, whatever its origin, had at this stage in the building's history nothing obviously to do with Norsemen or MacLeods, or with the sanctuary. It was now a place to which people resorted for cures of various kinds. Dymes went on: 'This saint was for cure of all theire wounds and soares.' Those who were unable to visit the church in person 'were wont to cutt out the proportion of theire lame armes or leggs in wood with the forme of theire sores and

The Eoropie church before restoration. © RCAHMS.

wounds thereof and send them to the Saint where I have seen them lying vpon the Altar in the Chappell'. This particular act of faith, no doubt followed sometimes with a cure, may be related to the belief in cures for 'lunatics' at the church and to the visits paid for the same healing purpose to certain wells in many places throughout Scotland. In addition there was a part of the church interior 'soe holy in theire estimation that not anie of their weomen are sufferred to enter therein. Anie woman with child dareth not to enter within the doores of the Chappell, but there are certaine places without where they goe to theire devotions'. Why men should be considered more worthy of entry to 'the holy of holies' is not explained, but the practice is perhaps not inconsistent with other aspects of life in male dominated societies not confined to the islands.

Another striking feature of Teampull Mholuaidh and its place in the community was, according to Dymes, its role as a location for 'merry meetings' such as those held at Galson. The people 'had two generall meetings in the yeare at this Chappell, the one at Candlemas [2 February] and the other at Alhollautide [Hallowe'en] where theire custome was to eat and drincke vntill they were druncke. And then after much dancinge and dalliance togeather they entred the chappell at night with lights in their hands where they continued till next morninge in theire devotions. The last tyme of theire meetinge was at Candlemas last'. The reverence with which people approached the chapel on these as well as on other occasions was evidently not lessened by the custom of merrymaking outside, but, as seems always to be the case, someone was at hand to disapprove - even in 1630:

'They were prevented of theire Idolatrous worshipp by a gent. whoe is a Minister in the Isle, who albeit the place was farr from his aboade and out of his Cure, hee mett them at theire Assembly in the Chappell where he begann first to reason with them, then to admonish them and afterwards to threaten them both with God His Judgments and the Lawes of the Realme, in somuch as divers of the better sort of them promised to forsake that wonted Idolatry of theires.'

MacKenzie was of the opinion that this visiting minister was probably 'Farquhar Clerk from Ui' [Eye].

In spite of such efforts to suppress, ancient custom persisted. Martin omitted Teampull Mholuaidh from his list but tells of a practice associated with what he called 'the Church of St. Mulvay", usually identified as Teampull

Mholuaidh. It was clearly given up for a while in the mid seventeenth century but was not forgotten.

'The Inhabitants of this Island had an antient Custom to sacrifice to a Sea-God, call'd *Shony* at Hallowtide, in the manner following: The Inhabitants round the Island came to the Church of St. *Mulvay*, having each Man his Provision along with him; every Family furnish'd a Peck of Malt, and this was brew'd into Ale: one of their number was pick'd out to wade into the Sea up to the middle, and carrying a Cup of Ale in his hand, standing still in that posture, cry'd out with a loud Voice, saying, *Shony, I give you this Cup of Ale, hoping that you'll be so kind as to send us plenty of Sea-ware, for inriching our Ground the ensuing Year:* and so threw the Cup of Ale into the Sea. This was perform'd in the Night time. At his Return to Land, they all went to Church, where there was a Candle burning upon the Altar; and then standing silent for a little time, one of them gave a Signal, at which the Candle was put out, and immediately all of them went to the Fields, where they fell a drinking their Ale, and spent the remainder of the Night in Dancing and Singing, etc.'

If 'the Church of St. Mulvay' was indeed that at Eoropie, as seems certain, then there was a limited choice of place for wading into the sea on the nearby Ness coast. One was on the west side at Tràigh Shanndaigh, but the more likely was at the east-facing Stoth where in a period of westerly wind seaweed can be abundant. The celebrations on returning from the shore were in the fields and the church interior witnessed only silent worship and a candle flame extinguished, yet again the ancient custom, perhaps the same as that which, according to Dymes, took place at 'Alhollautide', was the subject of disapproval.

'The next Morning they all return'd home, being well satisfy'd that they had punctually observ'd this Solemn Anniversary, which they believ'd to be a powerful means to procure a plentiful Crop. Mr. *Daniel* and Mr. *Kenneth Morison*, Ministers in Lewis, told me they spent several Years, before they could persuade the vulgar Natives to abandon this ridiculous piece of Superstition;

which is quite abolish'd for these 32 years past.'

Nearly two hundred years after Martin, the Free Church minister of Kilmartin in Argyll recollected hearing of a more recent invocation similar to the appeal to Shony. It was 'addressed to St. Brianuilt' and was 'gone through by a man whose grandson was well known to the writer.... Being scarce of manure for his land at the end of the sowing season, he went on the 15th day of May - old style - being St. Brianuilt's Day, to the point of a promontory, near which he lived, and shouted "Brianuilt, Brianuilt, send seaware send seaware!" The legend goes on to say that his prayer was speedily answered, but it was accompanied by such a tremendous snowstorm as caused the affair to be remembered for many a long day.' The minister, a Lewisman, had heard all this when in the island and probably when working in Ness.

The sanctuary, the meetings, Shony and the candles may have become matter of tradition a long time ago, but Teampull Mholuaidh retained its importance in the minds of Ness people who, in the 1790s, 'pay it as yet a great deal of superstitious veneration, and indeed some of them retain still a few of the Popish superstitions.' 'Popish' or not, one of these, the search for cures at the church, persisted for at least another century though it no longer involved the use of wooden limbs.

A description in 1792 was not very specific as to the type
of illness relieved in this way:

> 'Tiample Maloni, at Ness, is a large build-
> ing, and the architecture of a more modern
> date, which confirms the account of its being
> built by one of the first McLeods of Lewis. A
> superstitious veneration is still paid to it,
> and no burials are permitted within the
> verge of the ground that surrounds it. The
> country people send their friends that are
> long lingering in sickness, to sleep here of a
> night, where they believe the Saint grants
> them a cure, or relief by death. I have known
> an instance of this not long ago.'

In the 1890s Rev. Malcolm MacPhail confirmed the
discovery by the Ordnance Survey men that people came
to Teampull Mholuaidh from all parts of Lewis chiefly
'for the miraculous cure of insanity', and that in his own
time 'the rites and ceremonies' associated with that cure
were still remembered. 'One of my earliest recollections
in connection with the temple,' wrote MacPhail, 'was
one day, hearing people remarking that a young man,
whose mind happened to be unhinged at the time, had

been seen passing through the district in which I lived, in the custody of friends, on his way to "Teampull-Eoropie".' More details followed:

'It was even then believed by some that if one afflicted with insanity could be coaxed to sleep within the precincts of the temple, he was sure to be, at least, partially restored after a sleep there...

After arriving at the temple at dusk the patient was made to walk round the temple seven times "sunwise" - "deiseil" - and to drink water from the "Holy Well of the Teampull", and was then freely besprinkled with the same water; but unless the patient slept after this treatment, there could be no cure.

I was slightly acquainted thirty-five years ago with the individual in question. He was then quite sane; and, as far as I know, was so ever afterwards. If he is still living, he is a few years under eighty........'

It was MacKenzie's view that the 'Holy Well' was in fact

'St. Ronan's Well, close at hand', while after his walk and sprinkling with the well water the patient 'was then bound and left for the night on the site of the altar'. MacKenzie then concluded that because of its association with 'lunatics' the chapel was most probably dedicated not to St Moluag at all but to St Maelrubha, who was 'regarded as the special healer of lunacy', and to whose island shrine in Loch Maree in mainland Ross-shire 'lunatics' were also brought for a cure. However sixteen years later, in 1919, he had changed his mind on the subject and was in no doubt that the dedication was indeed to 'St. Molua'. Dedications and disapprovals apart, the belief in the curing powers of the chapel outlasted the weather-proof condition of the building and survived as the chapel itself decayed.

Restoration of the ruinous structure was carried out between 1910 and 1912 by 'enthusiasts' of the Episcopal Church and from time to time services have been conducted there. In 1933 it was written of the much altered Teampull Mholuaidh:

'Today it is a repository for a number of quaint relics. It contains an alms-box, a baptismal font, a bell, a sheep milking-pail, a sacristy, querns, a stone cross from North

Rona, a collection of Stone Age receptacles, and a canoe oar dug out of the peat-bogs near the village of Shader. Under the pulpit is a chest containing the vestments used during the very occasional services now held in this pre-Reformation place of worship.'

Most of the 'relics' have now been dispersed, some to the Ness Historical Society in whose premises in Habost they can be seen by visitors. But even though the present building, standing solidly amid the croft land, may be nothing like the first occupant of the site, the atmosphere of a mysterious past lingers on. Why, it may be asked, were so many beliefs and customs associated with Teampull Mholuaidh and so few with Teampull Pheadair in Swainbost and the other chapels? Did Teampull Mholuaidh serve as the early parish church of Ness? The dedication to St Moluag, if that was indeed correct, might indicate that the chapel was much older than the suggested fourteenth century and older than a building dedicated to St Peter, perhaps indeed older than the notion of a parish church.

Chapter 6

ST PETER'S CHURCH, SWAINBOST

Not being on a separate island the important church at Swainbost, still known as Teampull Pheadair, received no comment from Monro in 1549, but it appears in Martin's list of Lewis churches where it is called 'St. *Peter* in *Shanabost*'. Muir wrote that 'Except St. Columba, in the district of Ey, it is the largest of the Lewis churches, the external length being over 63 feet'. That it was still in use in the mid eighteenth century is confirmed in a report from the local minister on the parish of Barvas. He stated that the distance 'from Barvas to Swanabost another place for worship' was 12 miles. The parish church was at Barvas, and the other 'place of worship' in Swainbost was certainly the old Teampull Pheadair, close by the Swainbost river and only a short way from the sea.

Its size and evident role as the original pre-Reformation parish church of Ness give Teampull Pheadair pride of place among the ecclesiastical buildings north of Barvas and Stornoway in the early period of history, although it might be considered that the church of St. Moluag in Eoropie is a close challenger. Clearly of religious importance in the later mediaeval period, it is interesting to find that despite its Catholic association it continued to be used for public worship long after 1700 and that it was either better built or better maintained than the later parish church in Barvas. The parish minister in the mid 1790s, Rev. Donald MacDonald, described the two buildings in his day. The church of Barvas, a successor to the mediaeval Teampull Mhuire, was 'a perfect ruin' and needed urgent repair or replacement, while 'The one in the district of Ness, about 12 computed miles from the manse, an old Popish church, called St. Peter's, was enlarged and rebuilt last year; it is thatched with heath'.

A new Parliamentary church was built at Cross in the late 1820s and a parish of Cross, roughly equivalent to the old parish of Ness but now including 'the two Galsons', was separated from Barvas a short while later under its own minister, Rev. Finlay Cook. It is very probable that Teampull Pheadair was abandoned at this stage although meetings addressed by a 'reader' may have been held in part of the building for a little while longer. Twenty years later the Ordnance Survey found it in decay:

'The ruins of a Church, Situated on the margin of Amhuinn Shuainaboist. Attached to it is a graveyard which is the only one in the district of Ness. Three of its walls are

The ruins of St Peter's Church. © Comunn Eachdraidh Nis.

Still Standing, but the fourth has partly fallen in. Formerly it was the parish Church of Ness, and became a ruin in 1829. It is said to have been rebuilt in 1756, and to have derived its name from its first pastor, but when first erected is unknown.'

Tradition perhaps corrects the date of rebuilding to a time more consistent with Rev. MacDonald's remark that work on the church was carried out 'last year'. At any rate, in spite of what the Ordnance Survey heard in or about 1852, Angus Gunn, North Dell, an elderly man in 1870, said then that when 'Eaglais Pheadair' was built the roof for it was taken from the large teampull in Eoropie, and when it was lengthened, about 1795, the stones for the additional walling were brought from Teampull Tòmas [Thòmais] which stood only two or three hundred yards away. Angus remembered seeing Teampull Pheadair still roofed. Beams from that roof were in due course used in building an taigh-sgoile beag, the small schoolhouse, and they were possibly used again in its replacement, an taigh-sgoile dubh, the black schoolhouse. According to recollections in 1898 the last 'reader' in the church was a Morrison called Iain Clèireach, his family being known later as Clann Iain Chlèirich. It may be that there was a connection here with 'Murdo

Clerach in Galson', who was summoned to a meeting by the minister in June 1783.

The dedication, rather than being a memorial to the first pastor, was no doubt simply yet another to St Peter, of which there were several in the Western Isles including of course that at Shader. As for the age of the church it is no more certain than that of any other in northern Lewis, although in view of the tradition relating the removal of materials from the churches of St Moluag and St Thomas it should be more recent than these and therefore perhaps mediaeval, founded possibly as a church for a congregation rather than as a hermitage for a monk or two. Today Teampull Pheadair seems rather lonely and distant from the villages of Ness and the people who must have worshipped in it, but it must not be judged by appearances. In earlier centuries the line of settlement was much nearer the coast, as it seems to have been in Barvas, and the church was then only a short walk from the houses. Around the late seventeenth century a form of glebe was found from the lands of Habost, the territory of which village used apparently to come to the wall of the graveyard, for in 1852 the Ordnance Survey noted of Abhainn Shuaineaboist that 'In its course it separates the villages of Suainaboist and Tabost'. There was however some uncertainty as to whether the church was on

St Peter's Church. © Michael Robson collection.

Swainbost or Habost ground. Martin said it was in Swainbost, while Rev. MacDonald a century later called it 'St. Peter's in Habost'; but the latter may have hurriedly misread Martin's list which to some extent he repeated in his account of the parish. Today the pasture land of Swainbost machair extends some distance on the 'Habost' side of the Swainbost river.

An ancient religious association in the area near the mouth of the Swainbost river seems to be indicated by two placenames in the vicinity, Na h-Anaidean and Cnoc an Anaid, neither of them precisely located but both immediately reminiscent of the similar placenames near the site of the chapel at Shader, also dedicated to Peter. It may be therefore that at least part of the graveyard is very old indeed. Farquhar Murray of North Dell, and Alasdair [Alexander] Murray, Swainbost Farm, both of them buried at Teampull Pheadair, belonged to the 'Gobha' family of Murrays, the first of whom in Ness is said to have been 'An Gobha Gorm', 'the blue smith', who arrived from Caithness in the early seventeenth century. A table slab inscribed with the name of Alasdair, who died in 1857, lies between the church ruins and the riverside wall, and 'An Gobha Gorm' himself is supposed also to be buried in that lair. An ancestor of Roderick Morison, known as An Clarsair Dall, the Blind Harper, is reckoned to have been the third person to be buried in the graveyard, although this seems unlikely. He was Angus, fourth son of John Morison, the last of the original line of brieves or judges in Ness, who was killed by John MacLeod of Assynt about 1600. Angus himself was killed too in a feud with the MacLeods. His nephew was Mr Murdoch Morison, minister of Barvas and Ness in the 1640s.

It was once considered most unlucky to bury on the north

side of the church, but then Rev. John Macrae, who was inducted to the new church of Cross in 1833 and became known as MacRath Mòr, big Macrae, when looking for a place to inter one of his children, saw the empty area and made enquiries about it. He was told that 'tuathal' was unlucky. 'What nonsense,' he said, and so the child's grave there became an example to others. So ran the story anyhow, perhaps to illustrate some form of 'enlightened' dismissal of established superstition. A mound east of the church was said to have been the common grave of men killed in a battle nearby on the banks of the river; though much of the ground in this direction is rocky and not easy to use, an old man is reported to have said once to his neighbours while attending a funeral at Teampull Pheadair: 'Be sure to bury me so that my feet are in close contact with the rock on the east side of the graveyard that I may have a chance of rising before the old fellows.' No doubt there will be other stories relating to ground that lies so near the heart of earlier Ness history.

Burials in the old cemetery continued regularly even after 1922 when the present Habost graveyard came into use, for established loyalties remained and later tomb-stones point to the more recent interments. When it comes to age it is impossible to distinguish between the innumerable, small, rough stones that mark the graves of centuries. Thus generations of Catholic and Protestant persuasion have finally been laid to rest anonymously together. Comparatively few stones have inscriptions and these have all been recently recorded as accurately as possible, for behind the simple wording lie personal histories of great interest which are often preserved in family tradition. There too are some of the rare fragments of Teampull Pheadair's recorded past.

Chapter 7

ST THOMAS'S CHURCH

There is little known about the long-vanished Teampull
Thòmais, the church of St. Thomas, on the west Atlantic
coast of Ness.

According to Martin there was a 'church' of 'St. *Thomas*
in *Habost*' but Rev. D. MacDonald, writing in the 1790s,
said that Teampull Pheadair was in Habost and Teampull
Thòmais in Swainbost. The word 'in' here meant as usual
that the chapel was situated on the land or territory
pertaining to the village. MacDonald may have been
correct, or he may have been uncertain as to the line of
boundary between the two settlements. Around 1870
Angus Gunn in North Dell spoke of 'St. Tomas on Machair
Suainebost'. To confuse matters further the survey of
1914 found two churches of the same name, Teampull
Thòmais a quarter of a mile to the north-west of Teampull
Pheadair, and Teampull Thòmais 'pointed out by a local
informant' half a mile south of Eoropie and '3/4 mile
north-west of Lionel crossroads'. No remains were
visible in either case, and the conclusion must now be

that only one chapel had existed and that on the former site.

The Ordnance Survey description seems to contain the most accurate information. The name 'Teampull Thomais' applied to 'The site of an old Church, on the Sea-Coast, near the mouth of Amhuinn Shainaboist'. No-one in 1852 had seen a building there. 'It has been a ruin during the memory of the oldest man in the Lewis. Its Stones were used in building [i.e. lengthening?] Teampull Pheadair which is adjacent to it. It is situated on the Summit of a Small Knoll, but the date of its erection is unknown'.

The hilltop site on which Teampull Thòmais used to stand. © Donna Scott.

The 'Knoll' rises conspicuously above the sea's edge a little north of the Swainbost river. In the top of it there is a hollow, possibly surrounded by a rim of wall foundations. Down below is a 'small cove or fissure' recorded by the Ordnance Survey as 'Geodha Shroth', a name that never appeared on the map.

Chapter 8

ST PETER'S CHURCH, SHADER

Of the church Martin listed as 'St.*Peter* in *Shiadir*' there is little to be seen but enough to stir the imagination. In 1914 the remnants were described as 'grass-covered foundations' standing 'about 15 yards from the edge of the rock Craig Gille Phadruig' at the north end of the shore called Mol Eire. It was said then to have external measurements of 33 1/2 feet length and 16 feet 8 inches breadth, the structure having apparently consisted of 'a nave and a chancel'. The rock may have been named after a monk or holy man, a 'servant of Patrick or Peter', associated with the church.

The account of the site given in February 1852 by Thomas O Farrell for the Ordnance Survey supplies almost the only information about the burial ground at Teampull Pheadair. It seemed then to be more in evidence than the church itself.

> ' This is an old burying place with the site of a place of worship. There are upwards of a hundred years since any was buried in it except a sailor who was cast ashore here

about 40 years ago. There is a tale of an old woman of Shadir who was spinning <u>black</u> wool in one of the houses near the graveyard. It is said that a woman rose out of the grave and entered the house when the old woman was spinning her <u>black</u> wool. Without speaking a word to any of the inmates she attacked the poor old woman and cut off one of her fingers with her teeth. This unwelcome visit of the dead was attributed by the people to the black wool. Long after this there was no <u>black</u> wool spun in the night time in the village without having a small tuft of <u>white</u> wool tied on the top of the distaff. It is also

Recognising the exact church site is difficult due to the numerous wall foundations in the area. This view from the shore shows an ancient wall which has been exposed by erosion. © Donna Scott.

81

said that very few if any of the natives were buried in it after this occurrence. The site of the Church is pointed out by the natives around and only including the graveyard. There is no more than forty years since the Gable ends of it were standing.'

Surprisingly enough, in view of the story he had told, O Farrell concluded his account of the site with: 'There are no Traditionary Stories regarding either Church or Graveyard nor can any further information be collected regarding its antiquity etc.' His local informant was a John MacDonald living in Shader.

Near the church and burying ground there are other features with religious associations. Rudha na h-Anaid and the stones Clachan na h-Anaid, names denoting the presence of an ancient ecclesiastical centre, one of the many 'annats' in Scotland, lie to the north-east and south respectively, and Martin records a well of importance known by the name of a saint not usually found in the west:

'St.*Andrew's* Well in the Village *Shadar* is by the vulgar Natives made a Test to know if a sick Person will die of the Distemper he

The site of St Peter's Church, Shader. © Donna Scott.

83

labours under. They send one with a wooden Dish to bring some of the Water to the Patient, and if the Dish which is then laid softly upon the Surface of the Water turn round Sunways, they conclude that the Patient will recover of that Distemper; but if otherwise, that he will die'.

Chapter 9

ST BRIDGET'S CHURCH

On the slope of croftland above Allt Ghrunndail at Melbost and not far in from another stretch of shore called Eire is a small burial ground with the site of the church which Martin named 'St. *Brigit* in *Barove'*. This church, 'Teampull Bhrighid' on the Ordnance map, was said in 1914 to be 'now represented by an irregular grassy mound in an old burying ground, stones having been removed since 1888, when the land was given to crofters'. Small rough stones, apparently marking graves, jut up from the turf within what seems to have been an inclosure, and part of the site may have been used for dumping loose stones turned up nearby in the course of ploughing.

In 1852 not much more of the church existed than can be seen today:

'The ruins of a Church situated on the seashore at the North-East end of Eire. It has the appearance of the ruins of a hut, and resembles a pile of stones, more than the ruins of a Church. About 100 years ago the

85

interior was used as a burying ground; but there are no traditional stories regarding either Church or grave-yard.'

Removal of stones must certainly have contributed to the virtual disappearance of the church, whether it happened in immediately post-Reformation times, or in the nineteenth century when the nearby boundary wall of the Galson farm lands must have been built, or perhaps after 1888 and even as late as the 1920s when the farm was broken up and construction work took place at the well of St Bridget, Tobair Bhrìghid (Bhrìghde), a short distance from the chapel.

The remains of St Bridget's Church, Melbost. © Donna Scott.

Chapter 10

ST CLEMENT'S CHURCH

Martin gives probably the only record of a chapel in Ness called 'St. *Clemen* in *Dell*'. The dedication, an uncommon one in the islands, was therefore to St Clement, whose name is better known in its association with the church at Rodel in Harris. There is Tobair Chlèamain, Clement's Well, in the parish of Strath, Skye, and at Northton in Harris the great stretch of sands was called Tràigh Chlèamain, Clement's Strand.

The site of the church of St. Clement in Ness, perhaps once known as Teampull Chlèamain, is not now fixed with certainty. One clue seems to be that provided by Captain F W L Thomas in his article 'On the Duns of the Outer Hebrides'. Drawing largely on information supplied to him by Rev. Malcolm MacPhail, Thomas refers to a fort called 'Dun Cleamon' at a site 'now ploughed over' on 'Dail o Thuath', a name that he translates as 'South Dale' but which is correctly rendered into English as North Dell. The mention of ploughing might suggest that the site was in a field of the Dell farm, and if this were so then it may have been somewhere between Baile Glom and the Dell river in an area where there was also a well called Tobair Chlèamain. It is even possible that Thomas or his informant happened to change a church into a dun, but in any case the former presence of a dun and a well could possibly indicate the location of the church. There is a tradition that a church stood on the rising ground of Arnistean, above the shore.

Chapter 11

THE CHURCH AT GALSON

The church on the green terrace just above the sea at Galson is one of many ancient treasures found along that particular stretch of coast. There is some disagreement about the significance of the name. Martin called it '*Holy-Cross* Church in *Galan* ', but it is usually recorded in Gaelic as 'Teampull na Crò Naomh', and the uncertainty lies in how to express this name in English. Martin's version is the usual one, probably because it was the first, and this was accepted by T. S. Muir (1861), but 'Holy Fold Temple', the explanation given by the Ordnance Survey ten years earlier, has been preferred by some, and the Royal Commission report of June 1921 decided on 'the Church of the Holy Blood'. More interesting perhaps is Carmichael's account of the place, in which he compares the name to that of two wells in Uist - Tobair Crò Naomh. Here he translates the words as 'Well of the Holy Heart', and records that at the South Uist location 'All who drank of its refreshing and curative waters placed a votive offering in the cairn beside the well'. As for the church at Galson, Carmichael says that it was called 'Teampull Cro Naomh', in English Temple of the Holy Heart.

From Angus Gunn in North Dell Carmichael heard about the origin of the church:

'Tradition says that it was built as a "nasgadh deirce", vow-offering, by a Saxon who, when in peril in the North Sea [i.e. Atlantic ?], vowed that if saved he would build a Temple to Christ wherever he might be cast ashore. He was cast upon the wild coast of Gauslan [Galson], and built the temple on the spot where he offered up prayer for his deliverance.'

Teampull na Crò Naomh was ruinous probably long before 1800, but in William Daniell's 1819 illustration of 'Remains of a Temple at Galston, Isle of Lewis', it looks in much better condition that it is today. It seems that Daniell picked up part of a story about the place, for he remarked that 'It was visited till within these few years by many of the peasantry' and that 'At one of their merry meetings it was ascertained that a man had taken an indecorous liberty with a female; the hallowed purity of the temple was in consequence destroyed'. This suggests that the church may have remained in use until the late eighteenth century, and it is pleasant to think of 'merry meetings' taking place there.

At some point, perhaps around 1850, 'the tenant of the farm removed the stones of the temple to build a fold for his cattle'. When the Ordnance Survey men arrived in 1852 they found 'The ruins of a church on the sea shore, ...Its walls are about 5 feet high'. They heard no tradition about it, 'beyond, that it was much resorted to by Catholics in former times; So much so, that they came from all the adjacent islands, on a pilgrimage to it. It was built of Stone and mortar, with a loft'. And 'Attached to it is a grave yard in which are two vaults'. As at Teampull Pheadair in Swainbost the graveyard continued to be used long after the Reformation and burials still occur there.

The Daniell print of the Galson church. © Michael Robson collection.

BIBLIOGRAPHY

A.O. and M.O. Anderson (edits.)*Adomnan's Life of Columba*
[London 1961]
J. Brand *A New Description of Orkney, Zetland, Pightland-Firth and Caithness* [London 1703]
R.G. Cant *The Medieval Churches and Chapels of Shetland* Shetland Archaeological and Historical Society [Lerwick 1975]
R.G. Cant *'The Medieval Church in Shetland: Organisation and Buildings'* - in D.J. Waugh and B. Smith (edits.) *Shetland's Northern Links - Language and History* Scottish Society for Northern Studies [Edinburgh 1996]
A. Carmichael Manuscript Collection, Edinburgh University Library (Contains traditions from Angus Gunn)
A. Carmichael *Carmina Gadelica* (Vol. II)
[Edinburgh 1928]
R. Cochrane (edit.) *Report of an Excursion to the Western Islands of Scotland, Orkney ,and Caithness, June 1899* [Dublin 1900]
I.B. Cowan *The Parishes of Medieval Scotland*
Scottish Record Society Vol. 93. [Edinburgh 1967]
J.W. Dougal *Island Memories* [Edinburgh 1937]
Dymes - see W.C. MacKenzie (1903)
E.R. Lindsay and A.I. Cameron (edits.) *Calendar of Scottish Supplications to Rome 1418-1422*
Scottish History Society 3rd Series Vol. XXIII [Edinburgh 1934]
A.A. MacGregor *The Enchanted Isles: Hebridean Portraits and Memories* [London 1967]
A.A. MacGregor *Searching the Hebrides with a Camera* . [London 1933]
F. McGurk (edit.) *Calendar of Papal Letters to Scotland of Benedict XIII of Avignon 1394-1419* Scottish History Society 4th Series Vol. 13. [Edinburgh 1976]
I.F. Maciver 'A 17th Century "Prose Map" ' in F. MacLeod (edit.) *Togail Tir: Marking Time*
[Stornoway 1989]
C. MacKenzie 'An Account of some Remains of Antiquity in the Island of Lewis, one of the Hebrides' in *Transactions of the Society of the Antiquaries of Scotland* Vol. I. [Edinburgh 1792]

W.C. MacKenzie *History of the Outer Hebrides* (Includes 'Description of Lewis' by Captain Dymes 1630) [Paisley 1903]

W.C. MacKenzie 'Notes on the Pigmies Isle, at the Butt of Lewis, with results of the recent exploration of the "Pigmies Chapel" there' in *Proceedings of the Society of Antiquaries* Vol. 39 (1905).

W.C. MacKenzie*The Book of the Lews* [Paisley 1919]

J.M. MacKinlay *Ancient Church Dedications in Scotland* Non-Scriptural Dedications [Edinburgh 1914]

M. MacPhail 'Teampull Eoropie, Lewis' in *Oban Times* 5.11.1898; 'Teampull Ronain' in *Oban Times* 26.11.1898; 'Eaglais Pheadair' in *Oban Times* 3.12.1898

J. Marsden *Sea Road of the Saints: Celtic Holy Men in the Hebrides* [Edinburgh 1995]

M. Martin *A Description of the Western Islands of Scotland* 2nd Edition [London 1716]

W. Matheson (edit.) *The Blind Harper: The Songs of Roderick Morison and his Music* Scottish Gaelic Texts Society [Edinburgh 1970]

W. Matheson 'The Ancestry of the MacLeods' in *Transactions of the Gaelic Society of Inverness* Vol. LI [Inverness 1981]

Minutes of the Presbytery of Lewis Scottish Record Office CH2/473/1 & 2

John Morison (c. 1680) see I.F. Maciver

T.S. Muir *Characteristics of Old Church Architecture etc. in the Mainland and Western Islands of Scotland* [Edinburgh 1861]

T.S. Muir *Ecclesiological Notes on some of the Islands of Scotland* [Edinburgh 1885]

R.W. Munro (edit.) *Monro's Western Isles of Scotland and Genealogies of the Clans 1549* [Edinburgh 1961]

Ninth Report with Inventory of Monuments and Constructions in the Outer Hebrides, Skye and the Small Isles of the Royal Commission on Ancient and Historical Monuments and Constructions of Scotland [Edinburgh 1928] (Includes surveys dated 1914, 1921, 1924).

H.C. Nisbet and R.A. Gailey 'A Survey of the Antiquities of North Rona' in *The Archaeological Journal* Vol. CXVII [June 1962]

Ordnance Survey Name Books Scottish Record Office RH4/23/165

Reports of Ministers National Library of Scotland Adv. MS 16.1.7
Vol.V
M. Robson *(Rona:) The Distant Island*
[Stornoway 1991]
H. Scott *Fasti Ecclesiae Scoticanae*
[Edinburgh 1915-1928]
Sibbald's Collections National Library of Scotland Adv. MS 33.5.15
containing 'An Account of the Isles Hirta and Rona'
W.F. Skene *Celtic Scotland: A History of Ancient Alban*
[Edinburgh 1880]
A. Smith *An Eaglais Mhòr (The Large Church)*
[Ness 1992]
The Statistical Account of Scotland 1791-1799 edited by Sir John
Sinclair. Reprint Vol. XX The Western Isles [Wakefield 1983]
F.W.L. Thomas   'On the Duns of the Outer Hebrides' in
Archaeological Scotica Vol. 5 Part III [1890]
W.J. Watson *The History of the Celtic Place-Names of Scotland*
[Edinburgh 1926]